Broken Heart Healed

Aria Pestonji

BookLeaf Publishing

India | USA | UK

Presentation by *BookLeaf Publishing*

Web: www.bookleafpub.com

E-mail: info@bookleafpub.com

ISBN: 978-93-5761-238-8

First edition 2022

DEDICATION

Dedicated to anyone who has ever hurt me and
I have ever hurt.

ACKNOWLEDGEMENT

Thank you to those who inspired the poems and
those who inspired the poems' titles.
To Mum and Dad, thank you for always
believing in me.
This collection is inspired by the lyricism of
female artists like Taylor Swift, Olivia Rodrigo,
Maisie Peters, Billie Eilish, Kacey Musgraves
and Lorde, so thank you to them for their years
of supreme lyrical inspiration.

PREFACE

I have spent my entire childhood from when I was 6 to now, when I'm 18, seeking out drama, whether it was intentional or not. I spent a long time pretending I was the main character in the world and that nothing could ever be my fault. So when my relationship with the person I thought I would end up marrying blew up around the time of my 18th birthday, I knew I had to change the way I lived. And writing poems helped me do that.

I wrote most of these poems with no intention of anyone ever reading them. I wrote some while crying, some while cackling maniacally and some in a fit of rage. I reflect on the events of the past few years in my personal life and also in the world.

The titles of these poems, for the most part, are direct quotes of things people have said to me. Some run through my head constantly, others took some digging to find.

The process of putting this collection together was both traumatising and cathartic. What started as an aggressive F you to anyone who had ever hurt me, turned into a heartfelt apology to those I had hurt.

This collection is sassy, authentic, contradictory, honest and jarring, just like me.

Yeah that is quite weird [I.S.]

Every year I repeat the same story
The predictability is starting to bore me
Autumn, us outside, we're undefined
You get your wingman to close the blind
I've kissed him too, like I kissed you that night
But that will be my fault, not his - isn't that right?
We start dating and it's great
Talking on the phone, we stay up late
You say you want to know me better
You hold me close, write me a love letter
I tell you, all will eventually be revealed
But from the last one, I haven't healed
Passion and fun, it's all hazy
You still believe I'm the good kind of crazy
In October, we go to Halloscream
At the end of the night, we cuddle till we dream
Your friends warn you I'm a mistake
They say 'run far away from that manipulative snake'
But summer comes along, we heat up
Mix red wine and diet coke in the cup

Spend the day at the eastern beaches
In a bikini and everything is peaches
You call me baby, I call you snuggle bunny
You thought that was just you? Ha, that's funny
You say you're not like your predecessor
For starters, you're a better dresser
You make me feel safe and warm
And that's when you start to transform
Suddenly you don't want to know any more
Loving me has become a chore
We stay together and I don't know why
Maybe because all I do is try
December, our first time, you pinned up my arm
I flew to you and your grandparent's farm
I hate Christmas and I tell you why
But you say it will be better this time
New Year's kiss, you promise to stay
And you do, at least until Valentine's day
Something changes after our day of romance,
The fighting restarts, we snap out of our trance

Every man for themselves, but the girl is left
behind
Should've seen it coming but love left me blind
You said I was the most beautiful girl in the
school
I guess that changed when we moved to
Blackwattle
I say, 'please don't do this to me'

But all you want is to be free
I scream, 'what happened to us?'
But there's nothing left for us to discuss
I've become the villain of your story
Abandoned here in purgatory
For the last 4 Marches, I've been broken
by a guy, I trusted not to treat me like a token
Twice is a coincidence you could concur
But 4 in a row is strange to occur
But every March without fail
My heart is crushed and our love turns stale
In April, I peel myself up off the floor
And I ask myself, "how many more?"
Eventually, someone will actually stay
But until then, I'll see you next May

Duchess Fluffy Bunny of Fluffles

A spritz of perfume
Enough to make the memories loom
It takes me back to another time
When our love was in its prime

A letter written with so much love
Now you're impossible to get ahold of
The fluffy toy I hold close every night
I really do love it you were right

The ring symbolising your beautiful lies
Every move I made you'd criticise
The cherry made from the most delicate glass
The awkward interactions during class

I was meant to be your best friend,
How was I to know this is the way we'd end?
I could throw away the gifts and burn the photos
But I'd still be left like a wilted rose

She literally just won't eat [P.J.]

She crept into my life and told me pretty lies
She said everything would be better if I dropped
a size
But she failed to mention what I would sacrifice
With these bottomless goals, I was tantalized

She pushed away my family
Forced me to live life warily
Eventually, I lost all of my friends
With some, I never made amends

I broke down crying every night
There was no end to my pain in sight
She said it'd be fine if I lost more weight
I just had to get rid of what little I ate

I lost more control every day
I felt my life slipping away
There had to be more to life than this
There was so much I didn't want to miss

I didn't want to keep living with guilt

But it was scary destroying everything I built
I didn't want to keep living with shame
But eventually, she was something I overcame

I had to unlearn everything she taught
Work through every destructive thought
While I always try to silence her noise
She often returns with new ploys

She appears when I'm stressed
And when I'm getting dressed
She visits at all social events
And I remind myself of her malicious intent

They're just tired of supporting you with you constantly choosing to make bad decisions [A.A.]

To all the boys I've loved before
2 or 3 or maybe more
To all the boys I've pursued
And all the boys who've seen me nude
You might think I'm a vapid whore
But at least I'm not a bore
You say that this isn't empowering
But you seemed fine with it during my
deflowering
"I'll always be honest, no matter what"
That's what you said, guess you forgot
You want the picture of my crack
But it's too hard to snap me back
You say I'm an infuriating drama queen
It may be true but it's just mean

Making promises you can't keep
And you realise that you're in too deep
Why bother giving me that promise ring
If you're just going to leave when I say the
wrong thing
You push me to the brink
You judge me when I want to drink
You're only here for when it's fun
It gets a little complicated and you run
I've had my heart smashed into pieces
and each time my ability to trust decreases
I know it sounds like I'm really mad
but honestly, you weren't all that bad
I've made some very terrible decisions
If I could go back there would be revisions
And if I've learnt one thing from all the
Instagram blocks,
It's never date a guy wearing Birkenstocks

He's a keeper [K.P.]

I don't dump boys, they dump me
And even if I do, it's to set them free
I know you were too scared to break up with me
twice
If only *everyone* was that nice
My Grandma said he was good but you, I should
keep
Apparently, you thought I was too much upkeep

The place we met, so diplomatic
How could we turn so problematic?
I would have set myself on fire to make your
world brighter
Only to find it was you burning me down with
my own lighter

Too tough for you to be here on that day
I was too shocked to know what to say
Scared of what your dad would think
You were willing to let us sink

It was my goddamn birthday and you should've
been there
And you would've been if you cared

My family asked me about you
I smiled but I think they knew

I watched the door waiting for a surprise
All I got were watery eyes
I thought you couldn't disappoint me anymore
But somehow you provided an encore

One month after, it's your birthday
And I'm ready to pack my bags and stay
But you don't want me to come to Armidale
That was the moment I knew we'd fail

The smell of your stepmum's baked beans
reminds me of our show
Season 2 has come out, just thought you should
know
Without you, I can't watch Mr Bread
It's left on my list, so much unsaid

I tried so hard but you left me in the lurch
Out of spite, I might get married in a church
Children's titles, unused, such a shame
But I'll tell Lexie where she got her middle
name

Just like that I never returned
It's scary how quickly the tides turned
You went from the kindest boy I ever met

To a devil that I can't wait to forget

You couldn't even finish that song
You and your guitar strings strung me along
I really thought you'd be the one to stick
But it turns out you're just a… ugh not worth it

He's my oldest friend [I.R.]

You're mad at me, not him, because I'm your ex
I always loved you, I just needed sex
Regardless of what he might say
It really didn't happen at all that way
Everyone around him, he'll betray
But for him, you'll all give endless leeway
If I pulled half this shit, you'd go ballistic
And that's how I know you're all misogynistic
My rep makes it easy to let me be blamed
But one day you'll realise I've been framed
He can take the truth and twist it in his own way
Because nobody wants to believe what I have to
say
I know this time it wasn't all my fault
Even if that's not the stance of his fucked up cult
I'm not trying to start another fight
I do regret a lot that night
But I think you forget he was mine first
Guess you don't like it when the situation is
reversed

You're the most feminist person I know, don't ever doubt yourself [D.T.]

I'm a slut but he's a chad
She's a bitch but he's rad
The stark difference in vocabulary
Is a weight that women have to carry
They get away with things we never could
It's all chalked up to boyhood
"Girls mature faster,
But treat him like your master"
"He's mean so he must have a crush,
Suck it up and just hush"
"Yeah he's a dick but he's always been like that,
He's one of the boys, we gotta have his back"
But why can't I be treated the same
I'd love to not have to take any blame
He gets taught his destiny is to lead

But her only purpose is to breed
Straight white men in power, they don't care
That women aren't getting their fair share
And when we demand we get treated with
equality
They whine and say we have it so easy
We call men simps when they treat women well
But when they treat us like shit we're told not to
tell
"Women are caring mothers by nature"
Your fake science should stay out of legislature
These positive attributes are not used to
empower
They're used to defend our lack of power
When the headmistress pulls students and staff
out of class
To spend an hour defending an ass
Telling us that there's been no proof
That should reveal the disappointing truth
The system wasn't made for us to thrive
It doesn't care if we're dead or alive
We need a new system that feeds us all
But first, this one needs to take a fall

To my younger self

Focus less on being smart and more on being
kind
Doing nice things will make you happier, you'll
find
Drama won't make your life more fun
It will just leave you without anyone

Tell Mum and Dad you love them every day
There is no need to keep pushing them away
They will always be there, just tell them what
you need
You don't need to grow up with so much speed

Harness that passion and persistence into light
Know that it's okay to not always be right
Choose love over fear at every turn
From every mistake make sure you learn

Never be ashamed of who you are
but you don't need to take it so far
You don't need to keep proving you're worthy of
love
Life works out without needing to force the
glove

I'm so sorry for the way that I treated you
You're scared and confused and you can't break
through
The world is big and scary
And you feel trapped and wary

You deserved better
and so I'm writing this letter
to tell you I know you needed protection
instead, you got constant self-rejection

So, dear younger me
I promise you're plenty
Don't lose that enthusiasm
But maybe lose the sarcasm
Good thoughts, good words, and good deeds
That's the way to go, I concede

You're so excited you forgot a space [H.M.]

An elusive concept tearing us apart
Delaying the inevitable when you break my
heart
To think, to reconsider, to be alone
An excuse not to pick up your fucking phone

How you left me without actually leaving
Should have known to start the grieving
So easily you abandoned me at the depths of my
despair
Treat me like shit but still claim to care

You ran away so fast you won the race
Threw me away like a mistake to erase
Well that was a slap in the face
So fuck you and fuck your 'I need space'

"Maybe you didn't cheat, but you're still a traitor"

You convinced me that this was okay
She'll never know, I hear you say
And while that might be true
There's no way to justify what we're about to do
Down a few glasses of wine
And I think, maybe it's fine
I'm reading we're going into lockdown
I look at you and know exactly what I'm doing now
A moment I thought I'd always wanted
A guilty mistake that has left me haunted
I have a certain reputation
Now I'm living up to the expectation
10 seconds later and we're done
For the hurt it could cause, I'd hoped for more fun
We say we'll see each other in 2 weeks
And after that, we never speak
Justified it by saying I hate her
But that doesn't change that I'm a traitor

I stopped talking to you because you were toxic [E.A.]

Friendships ending has always felt so strange
By the time you realise, it's too late to change
Losing friends crushes your soul
Especially when you know you were the asshole
It's crazy to me how quickly things switch
Good people turn into a witch
A friend for life, I would assume
Until I threw up in her bathroom
The girl I thought I'd always hate
About to be my roommate
But that was all misogyny I internalised
Now I look at her and I'm just mesmerized
My best friend saved my life
Only to stab me in the back with her knife
Didn't give you a cigarette light
So of course that meant a 2-year fight
You make a mistake and people choose sides
Leading to a group divide
You can't really call it that when it's 12 against one
No one defended me - that was fun

But I was always looking for the next best thing
Missed what was right in front of me
Friends who would've stayed by my side
If their needs I hadn't denied
And I hate that I threw us away
I wish that I called you on your birthday
I expected unconditional loyalty
But I didn't deserve to be treated like royalty
Built walls and expected you to knock them
down
You couldn't so I was alone in my formal gown
And every friend I have has someone closer
Talking about my feelings, ugh, nothing grosser
So I told myself that everyone left me
But I didn't give them a choice really
I wouldn't have been friends with myself
So how could I expect anything else

"Who am I? That's one secret I'll never tell."

I want to explore every inch of this world
But I want to stay in bed all day, curled
I'd love to accomplish every one of my dreams
But honestly, that's quite extreme
How can I read every book ever written?
There's never enough time for what I want to fit
in
I want to learn all the facts to be wise
And win every accolade, award and prize
I want the love, the loss - the highs and lows
And with every step to feel myself grow
Feel every emotion, the bad and the good
Do everything I know that I could
I want to be everyone's muse
but at the end of the day know it's you that I'd
choose
I want to feel the surge of an adrenaline rush
Be inspired by every stroke of the brush
I want to be the brightness in a world of dark
An angel who leaves her powerful mark

I want who I am to remain an unsolvable
mystery
but I also want to imprint on history

She doesn't like what you're doing to me [I.R.]

Your dad came into my work today
I was speechless, didn't know what to say
He didn't seem to recognise me
I was hurt but that was lucky
I suppose your parents always loved her more
It's fine I'm not keeping score

I keep drafting messages to your mother
I never send them, I don't want to be a bother
We were meant to go drinking after my birthday
But I haven't heard from her since that day
You're so obsessed with your dad, you don't see
it
But one day you will and I'll be acquitted

Your mum was the catalyst of our demise
She wants to be the only woman in your eyes
Said we were too young to know what love was
In her defence, that was probably the menopause

I complain a lot about my parents
But one thing they did better is quite apparent
They never tried to influence who I dated
And trust me, some of you they hated

You can be anything you want to be [C.P.]

What are my goals in life?
To be a mother and a wife?
To save the world or just myself?
To write a book that lands on everyone's shelf?

Is a goal the end or just a checkpoint to cross?
Does all the hard work end when you're the boss?
Or will you never really be finished?
Every accolade left diminished?

Can I succeed and stay who I am?
Or do I have to transform into a 'ma'am'?
Can I exude a soft warm glow
and be a boss who runs the show?

Can I be a doting mother to my children
While still raking in the millions?
City living and a rustic country house

loungewear, hair up and perfectly manicured in a
business blouse

Can I be everything I want to be?
Or do I need to sacrifice what makes me happy?
I may make mistakes; stumble and fall,
But I'll never let that stop me from having it all

Hey thanks for having us over, it was a really fun night (especially the yoga at 5am) [T.H.]

It was a good thing we had going
But good things rarely last
I'd hoped we make it longer
Now it's all in the past

I know we all dated within the group
There were more than a couple coups
But we had a lot of fun
Pool parties in the sun

I miss our Friday afternoon
I'm sad it had to end so soon
And I miss complaining about China Town
While my 'much better' suggestions were
knocked down

I miss our 700 group chats
One for each of our pointless spats
I miss having you over at mine
And being judged for my diet coke and wine

Our grotty lunch spot in Balmain
I'd do anything to be there again
The Darling Harbour swing
Karaoke, G6 you'd sing

I miss watching movies I don't care about
I miss the group leader and his sidekick with all
their clout
I miss spending hours planning simple events
I miss organising Secret Santa presents

And some of you may still be friends
But nobody likes the way that story ends
Fragments broke off, 'the group' dissipated
Individuals' morality heavily debated

I asked you all a while ago what you miss
To say that ended well would be remiss
We could have gone without her little outburst
But I got some cute information first

You miss the Maccas on George street

Parties at mine, in the heat
Spice Alley late at night
Removing me as admin; hurtful but alright

Every single climate change march we're having a sesh [C.M.]

Over the bridge, far from town
Stood a tree peering down
It begged the question, 'Who was here before?'
'And who will arrive forevermore?'
The tree compares the now to the past
It exclaims that things "have changed so fast
It feels like only yesterday
Children were here, laughing as they play
Seasons used to come and go
And I could watch the beautiful creatures grow
As I look up at the towering skyscraper
I wonder if I'm next to be turned into paper
All my friends have been taken for bank
statements and contracts
Without a second thought about their impacts
And I think about the families that have come
and gone

They picnicked under me as I shaded them from
the sun
And I ponder the family who will come next
Will they laugh and talk or will they just text
Will they remember to put their rubbish in the
bin
Or will they leave it to reabsorb into my skin
I can no longer withstand the droughts, storms
and hurricanes
But I hope you learn from my remains"

Let it go [C.C.]

Let it go, people move on. Your toxicity and consistent victim act are boring. I'm sorry you felt the need to start something where there simply wasn't any need to.

It's been over 3 years but I can't stop myself
I see you at a club and rage fills my body
I give you the middle finger
It doesn't make it better
It just makes me feel stupid
I've got to let it go

It's been over 2 years but I can't stop myself
I see you after our last exam and I have to say
something
But you've moved on and trust me I get it
She's the loveliest person
And I bet your mum likes her more
I've got to let it go

It's been over a year but I can't stop myself
I message you 'hey'
You just respond 'what do you want?'
Then I see you were at Ikea with her
I didn't know you were together

I've got to let it go

It's been months but I can't stop myself
I see you checking my stories
But you removed my follow
I want to know how you're doing
But I'm scared you're doing fine
I've got to let it go

Ride or Die [M.J.]

Patting my back when I'm feeling anxious
Making breakfast so delicious
Getting me flowers
Staying on the phone for hours

Squeezing my hand so I know you're there
In a way that no one could compare
You came with me to Broadway before school
Protected me from ridicule

Told your mean friends it was enough
Stayed when it was getting rough
Held up my head because I asked
Made sure I never felt outcast

Photos printed and framed
Letters with your love proclaimed
Walk before extension math class
Laughing while lying on the grass

In the swings in the park
Talking till it stops being dark
Succeeding when I never thought I could
Always looking to find more good

Food that is delicious
Being ambitious
Shopping till I drop
Dancing to trashy pop

A babies smile
Their laugh making it all worthwhile
A whole room laughing at my joke
Drinking up my diet coke

I want a life basking in the sun
Not worrying about which of us won
I can't waste more time trying to destroy
I have to keep choosing joy

I adore the expensive perfumes and gorgeous
rings
But I much prefer the little things

There's that word again [S.P.]

Growing up; moving out
Feeling confident; not a single doubt
You're scared I'm underestimating this
Scared I am going to crumble into the abyss

But the only reason I am capable
Is because you taught me I am unbreakable
Raised me to always persevere
Never be stopped because of fear

Showed me how to love
How to rise above
I've been eighteen since I was three
Because you raised me so responsibly

Stood by me even when I was wrong
Even when we didn't get along
Loved me when I said I hated you
You know that could never be true

Homework helpers, delicious meal makers
There for me through all the heartbreakers

Supported me when you didn't agree
Never stopped me from being me

Even when you got Roby
And tried to make me feel like a Toby
I've always known you loved me borstest*
It's getting tattooed, despite your protest

Travelled me across the world
Held my hair back while I hurled
The perfect example of soulmates
One I strive to emulate

Everything I will ever be
Is because of everything you've given me
I owe you a debt of gratitude
Love, your favourite and most valued

*best, most and more

You can't act like the victim here [E.H.]

Exes friends and friends exes
Not something one flexes
Destroying friendships mine and others
All I did was steal another's

Justified it a million times
Never caught for my crimes
He was right; it's not empowering
But I smiled while they were scouring

It shocks me I wasn't punched in the face
You would've had a solid case
I have plenty of excuses
But they don't change the killer bruises

I was drunk, lonely, sad?
Wanted to hurt you, I was so mad?
Only thinking of how it would affect me
Hedonism to the nth degree

I wished you good luck before that exam
But I should have told you how sorry I am
You were both 16 and deserved better
Instead of saying thank you I held a vendetta

I'm the only common denominator
Consistently the drama perpetrator
And you may have been insolent
But I am not innocent

I Love You

I once believed love would be burning red
That's what Taylor Swift once said
We both realised real love is gold
And we don't have to stay in the cold

I don't want to get hurt anymore
And I can't fight another war
I want a love that's warm and filled with light
Not one that's just a constant fight

When you're life burns to the ground
And there's no hope to be found
That's when you find your power
To grow into a bright-eyed flower

Focus on the rainbow that comes after the rain
Make something beautiful out of all the pain
Like a phoenix from the ashes, rise
Ignore the petty rumours and malicious lies

Never settle for the first version
Always strive to be a better person
While you're working on getting out of the
cocoon
Don't be afraid, you'll blossom soon

To be loved is to be known
I have reaped what I have sown
To be hurt is to have grown
Now I have to learn to be alone.